SECRETS OF USER-SEDUCTIVE DOCUMENTS

Wooing and Winning the Reluctant Reader

by

William Horton

 society for technical communication

ISBN 0-914548-96-4

STC 172-97

Society for Technical Communication

901 N. Stuart Street, Suite 904

Arlington, VA 22203-1854

(703) 522-4114

stc@stc-va.org

CONTENTS

1

WOO AND WIN THE READER

An unread document communicates nothing. It answers no questions, enables no action, solves no problems. A document must do more than allow access to information. It must compel reading and understanding and action. It must seduce the reader. From *The Iliad* to *Don Giovanni*, from *Little Women* to *As the World Turns*, seduction is a common literary theme. This booklet employs seduction as its organizing metaphor for the task of motivating reluctant readers of technical documents. Borrowing from pop sociology, it demonstrates seductive techniques to ensure that your document is read, understood, and acted upon.

The need to seduce

Dazzled by flashy technology, habituated to rock-music videos, and pressured for ever-greater productivity, users of technical products just don't read documents the way we writers wish they would. Documents that are merely polite or friendly don't do the job for audiences who are bored, busy, and sometimes hostile. These audiences must be *seduced* into reading.

To communicate with busy people

There is a rebellion in the land. Users of computers and other complex products refuse to read their manuals. They ignore the multimedia tutorials. They fume. They rant. They mangle their data. They simply won't spend the hours it takes to find the one fact they need among 900 pages or screens of solid text. And rumors have it that the rebellion is spreading to users of automobiles, microwave ovens, and even tricycles.

It is a sad fact of life that users don't read and memorize instruction and reference manuals cover to cover. If they read at all, it is to find a few specific facts. If they find these facts quickly, they are satisfied and put the manual aside. If they don't find the facts quickly, they are frustrated and also put the manual aside–for good!

For electronic documents, the situation is worse. Such documents seem subject to the *skydiving syndrome*: if your first attempt is not totally successful, you tend not to try again. Users often avoid online Help because they "tried it four years ago and it didn't work."

To quell this rebellion against reading, we must learn to create instructional and reference documents that people use—*even if they don't read them*. We have to confront the number-one complaint about most technical documents: It takes too long to find what you're looking for. Taking a multimedia tutorial evokes the same guilt as a time-squandering videogame.

On the job, users of technological products and information focus on the tasks they are trying to perform or the problems they are trying to solve. Burdened with personal problems and other demands on their time, most feel, perhaps rightly, that they have better things to do with their time than to read. "Hey, anybody know how to send a file to the printer?" they ask coworkers rather than consult the document.

They feel pressed to produce, not to read. Reading on the job is not always a sanctioned activity, even if the book is a manual or a help file. "Put that book aside and get to work!" nags the work-ethic demon.

Faced with a question about how to operate a piece of equipment, users evaluate their alternatives for proceeding and pick the most congenial one. Ask yourself what you do when you can't figure out how to do something with your word processor or computer. Usually these alternatives include the following:

- Try something and see what happens.
- Ask another user.
- Call the manufacturer.
- Quit and go home.
- Read the manual.

Generally, we choose the solution that yields the fastest answer. Unfortunately for the well-being of the equipment and the mental serenity of the user, reading the document often comes in dead last.

We must create a new type of technical document, one that answers questions in a hurry and gives quick relief. To produce such documents, we must take on the role of time managers for our readers. We must recognize that for most technical products

the cost of learning to use the product far surpasses the purchase price. We must engineer documents that do not waste users' time. We must produce documents that get them back to productive work without frustration or delay.

To avoid post-sale betrayal

Another reason for making workaday documents seductive is to prevent post-sale betrayal, or the feeling a customer gets after buying a product based on glib promises and glossy four-color brochures. The Armani-suited sales rep is nowhere to be found, and the manufacturer's toll-free number proves to be a not-so-hot line. It is then that the customer confronts the document: 500 pages of matrix-printed and photocopied gobbledygook, devoid of illustrations and humanity. Who can blame the user for being skeptical, hostile, or in some other state of mind not pleasantly disposed toward the manufacturer, the product, or the document? No wonder three simple words, *some assembly required*, strike fear into the hearts of millions of parents on Christmas morning.

To prevent disaster

Three Mile Island. The Space Shuttle Challenger. Bhopal. The Cali airline crash. These words evoke painful, perhaps angry, memories of disasters that were devastating to material, equipment, technological progress, national pride, and, worst of all, human life. In the intense investigations by government panels and the news media following these tragedies, two painful facts emerged:

- Ignorance contributed to or directly caused the disaster. Time and time again responsible managers grimly admitted under intense questioning that they would have acted differently had they been fully aware of the dangers. The *Report of the Presidential Commission on the Space Shuttle Challenger Accident* revealed that:

  ... the reporting system was not making trends, status, and problems visible with sufficient accuracy and emphasis.

  Likewise, the Presidential Commission studying the accident at the Three Mile Island nuclear power plant concluded that the behavior of the operators of the plant, as they disabled one after another of the various automatic safety systems before these systems could bring the crisis under control, revealed that they didn't understand the fundamental physics of how their plant worked.

- **The problems were well documented.** Memos, reports, and manuals unearthed during the investigations pointed out the problems and associated potential for disaster in each case. *The New York Times* reporter on the Bhopal refinery chemical spill that killed thousands cited the safety procedure manual (the infamous orange book) in his investigations and found it complete and understandable. An incorrect command typed into an onboard navigation computer sent an American Airlines flight into the side of a mountain in Columbia. Yet the instruction manual for the system described the command clearly and correctly.

To combat voluntary illiteracy

What went wrong, then? Why did those with power to prevent these disasters not act? In Bhopal, part of the problem was illiteracy among workers. But that was not the problem at Three Mile Island or Cape Canaveral. "Nor is it the problem for my manual, my proposal, or my brochure," you might protest.

I would argue that it *is* the problem. Illiteracy and subliteracy are certainly severe problems, but I'm talking about a special kind of illiteracy. It is not that users of technical products *can't* read but that they *won't* read. For whatever reason, those who need to know don't read and understand vital information.

I don't want to debate the writer's ethical responsibility in all this. But I would like to suggest that merely putting the facts down in print does not let the writer off the hook. Writing is a social act, and our responsibility goes beyond putting words on paper. It requires putting people in action. Sometimes we must seduce them into action.

Not just for sales and marketing fluff

When I suggest that hard-core business documents should be seductive, I often get the objection: "We do technical documents, not marketing fluff."

Yet the same companies are paying US$35 to $50 for customer-support hotlines to answer questions that are already answered in user's manuals and help files—only nobody reads the document.

Seduction is not sexist. It is an equal opportunity employer. Men seduce women. Women seduce men. Men seduce men. Women seduce women. Ideas seduce them both. Properly designed documents can seduce reluctant readers.

Two trends are common in usability testing and focus groups—users rarely use technical documents spontaneously, but those who do are often pleasantly surprised. "I never thought to try the manual. Wow, it's actually in English, not gobbledygook," volunteered one test subject who started reading the manual after exhausting all other possible solutions to a problem.

Beyond user-friendliness

What do I mean by *seductive*? In this context, seductive does not mean erotic or sexy or even beautiful. This booklet will not improve your romance novel. It will not teach you to write for *Cosmopolitan* or *Playboy*. We mean something different. A dictionary definition might run something like this:

se • duce (sih-doos) tr.v. -duced, -ducing, -duces.
  1. To lead away from proper or conventional conduct; lure into wrongful behavior.
  2. To induce to have sexual intercourse.
  3. To attract; win over.
  4. To beguile or entice into a desired condition or state.
[From Latin *seducere*, to lead away: se, apart + ducere, to lead.]

We are not talking about definitions 1 and 2 but about 3 and, to some extent, 4. We want to attract our readers' attention and win their sympathy. We want to entice the reader into a state of informed action. We want to lead the reader away from ignorance and toward understanding. In the context of technical communication, seduction means:

the effective use of readers' natural curiosity and intelligence to ensure that the document gets read, understood, and acted on.

In the courtship rituals of most cultures—and many species for that matter—someone ... or some thing ... must take the lead and initiate wooing.

> No one can write decently who is distrustful of the reader's intelligence, or whose attitude is patronizing.
> — E. B. White

Passive friendliness is polite and takes care not to offend, but it sometimes takes active seduction to get the potential reader to actually read the documents. The difference between passive friendliness and active seduction shows up in the way we phrase goals and purposes of the document:

Friendly document	Vs	Seductive document
enables to do		gets to do
enables to find		shows
presents clearly		teaches
makes a case		convinces
is readable		gets read

Notice the subtle difference: Writers of friendly documents leave responsibility for finding information to the reader, but writers of seductive documents assume full responsibility for making the reader notice, understand, and act on the information.

> There is nothing so captivating as new knowledge.
> — Peter Mere Latham

Friendliness is a response, seduction an act. Friendly documents allow access to information—if the reader is motivated and tries to find it. Seductive documents go further and supply the motivation. In other words, user-friendly documents try hard, but user-seductive ones accomplish results. User-friendliness invites reading; user-seductiveness compels it.

R. E. S. P. E. C. T.

According to the lowest-common-denominator theory favored by some teachers of technical writing, we should write as if the reader were "an absolute idiot." Such advice is idiotic. Our audiences are not moronic drones but intelligent and curious adults (people like us) who are long on tasks to perform but short on time. The growth of science magazines and television programs over the last few years demonstrates that people do want to learn about lasers, electronics, space flight, computers, and other technical advances.

Technology can intrigue, interest, and motivate readers if we, as writers and document designers, do our part.

Set seductive objectives

Here's a typical charter for a business document:

> The User's Guide will clearly present procedures for operating the ZipGlop 3000.

Look at all the weasel words and notice how it abdicates responsibility to the reader. A more seductive document might result from a charter like this one:

> Within three days, eighty-five percent of new users will be able to perform their work with the ZipGlop 3000 and calls to customer support will be less than half those for comparable products.

Look at the charter or purpose statement for a document you are producing. Is it seductive? If not, rewrite it.

2

FLIRT WITH THE READER

Seduction begins with flirtation. Flirtation is far from casual. It has the serious goal of catching attention and making acquaintance. It is the first step in winning acceptance. To make our technical documents effective, we must make readers aware of our documents and ensure that they feel comfortable browsing our documents' pages. We must make the document flirt with the reader first.

Make your availability known

People don't read documents they are unaware of. The first step, then, is to make potential readers aware that the document is available.

I once worked on a project to deliver the equivalent of 1700 pages of documents as a Help system. Months after release, we found that almost no customers were using the Help system. We put a Help entry on the main menu. We mentioned it in the getting started manual. We told the training instructors about Help. We built it, but they did not come. Not until we completed a full-scale advertising campaign to tell users that Help existed and it was great.

Advertise

In most cultures people advertise their availability or nonavailability for romantic rela-

tionships. They do it with a flower behind the ear or a wedding ring. They do it with a style of clothing or a personal ad in a newspaper.

Unknown documents get few readers. Merely writing and publishing documents is not enough if potential readers are not made aware of the document and told how to obtain a copy.

Publicize the document

Don't hide your documents from potential readers. For every document plan a public relations campaign to get the word out. Use the techniques in the accompanying checklist to better publicize your document.

Checklist for publicizing documents

- ☐ Include them on your company's price list along with other products

- ☐ Issue a special publications catalog

- ☐ Mail announcements of new documents to existing customers

- ☐ Send news releases announcing new documents to trade magazines and journals

- ☐ Exhibit your documents at conventions and trade shows

- ☐ Use them in training classes and as supplements to self-instructional materials

□ Donate copies to users' groups and technical libraries

□ Publish descriptions of the documents in customer newsletters

□ In each document, mention related documents, even those available from other organizations

□ Mention them on your Web site. Include links to a quick-order page

Tell readers how to order a copy

Don't do a halfway job. Make sure the reader gets all the information necessary to obtain a copy of the document.

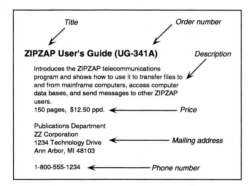

Give the reader:

□ Exact title and order number.

□ Description of the document in enough detail so readers can decide whether it answers their questions.

□ Where to place an order: mailing address, phone number, e-mail address, and Web site.

□ Price of the document.

Hang out in the right places

Another way to make readers aware of the document is to place it where they will be able to find it.

If the document is packaged with the product, ensure that it is placed atop the product. The user should see it first when opening the box, especially if the document is needed to unpack and set up the product. Nothing is more useless than unpacking instructions that the user discovers only after unpacking the product and possibly inflicting self-injury or damaging the product in the process.

I once worked on a product where the box designers put the instructions for unpacking and setting up the unit under a 90-lb computer. Fortunately we were able to revise the design so the unpacking instructions started on the top lid of the box.

You could take our solution even further and put instructions on the outside of the box to show readers how to find the document.

It is important that users perceive the document as part of the product. Toward this end you can include the document in product photographs for trade magazine articles, brochures, and advertisements.

Often computer hardware and software are exhibited and demonstrated at trade shows and user group meetings. Why not take along some documents as well? They make excellent sources of technical information for those interested in more details than are in brochures or sales demos.

For Help and other electronic documents, they know it's there, right? Alas, electronic documents can be invisible documents, even when their icons squat squarely on the desktop. To advertise electronic documents:

☐ Include a Help menu with enticing entries.

☐ Put buttons as reminders on dialog boxes.

☐ Advertise Help and tutorials on installation screens between diskette swaps.

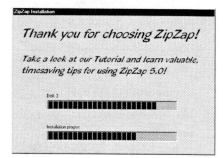

☐ At the end of the installation process, start up Help for the user and display the topic on using Help.

☐ Teach how to use Help in all classes, CBT lessons, tutorials, and guided tours. In Help refer users to CBT and tutorials.

☐ Include screen snapshots of Help in sales brochures and data sheets. Show electronic documents as a routine part of sales demos.

☐ Mention Help and CBT on your Web site and let users download standalone copies.

Especially for Web sites

To get people to your Web site:

- ☐ Register with Web-directory services. For a complete list, go to `www.yahoo.com` and search for "Web announcement services".

- ☐ Include the URL on all your business materials: letterhead, business cards, brochures, pencils, coffee mugs.

- ☐ Mention it in all marketing, training, and support documents. I saw **www.FedEx.com** spelled out in flowers on the embankment of the main highway between the airport and downtown in Toronto.

- ☐ Include it in your e-mail signature.

- ☐ Send out a news release (paper and electronic) to associations and publications that serve your industry.

- ☐ Post informative, modest announcements to relevant Internet newsgroups.

But take care. If you attract too many informational joyriders, traffic can overwhelm your server thereby giving poor service to everyone and discouraging access by your customers or real target audience.

Dress for seduction

The next step in flirting is to catch and hold the reader's attention. In *Dress for Success*, John Molloy methodically documented the effect of a person's dress on first and lasting impressions. In fact, *Time* magazine called him a "wardrobe engineer." We can perform similar wardrobe engineering for a document by designing the cover and spine to catch the reader's attention and clearly identify the subject.

Colorful cover and spine

Office and factory environments often seem black, white, and shades of gray. Like the bright mating plumage of a tropical bird, a splash of color stands out and compels attention. The same applies to documents. A stripe or swatch of color makes bookcase wallflowers stand out.

There are some books of which the backs and covers are by far the best parts.

— Charles Dickens

Use a distinctive color, not necessarily a bright color. One company surveyed its customers' offices to find out the color of its competitors' catalogs. The company then made its own catalogs a contrasting, distinctive color. When the competitors' catalogs were green, its were orange. Next year, when competitors' catalogs had switched to orange, its were a tasteful blue.

A four-color cover can be expensive to produce. Consider some less expensive alternatives:

- Print the cover in blends of two colors.

- Bind the document in a loose-leaf binder with pockets for a slide-in cover and spine. For small quantities, print the color cover and spine using an inexpensive color-photocopy process.

Put title here

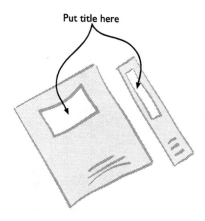

- Print the cover in an ink color other than black—dark blue, for example.

- Print the cover on colored paper.

- Preprint generic corporate covers in one color. Then print the title of the document and other information in a second color.

The cover should look as good as the best page inside—but not a whole lot better. A lavish, four-color cover sets expectations that a black-on-white, text-only interior cannot live up to.

Especially for electronic documents

For electronic documents, the "cover" is the splash screen or main menu. The cover of an electronic document performs a different purpose than that for a magazine or book. Since the user sees the cover only after selecting to start up the document, you have less need to sell the document or its subject matter than to direct the reader to specific content. The cover of an electronic document is not to arouse interest but to preserve it.

Especially for Web sites

The cover of a Web site is its Home page. Take care that your "cover art" does not make the page too slow to download.

- ☐ Use fewer colors in graphics. If you only need four colors, do not save your graphics at 24-bit color depth.

- ☐ Use smaller graphics. Crop graphics tightly, especially if surrounded by borders of the same color as the background color

- ☐ Rely on typography and background color to give the page a unique, interesting look.

Striking cover graphic

Like it or not, readers do judge a book by its cover. If the cover looks boring, readers assume the innards are boring, too. The myth perpetuates itself because they never bother to examine the contents.

Use pictures

Covers cry out for pictures. Not only do pictures draw the eye, but they are retained in memory better than the sound-alike titles of most documents. Several types of graphics are useful on covers:

- **Person using the product**. Nothing is more visually seductive than a human face. The face should express satisfaction with the product.

- **Photograph of the product**. Show the product in action or else keep the photograph simple.

- **Line drawing of the product**. The line drawing should be simple, clean, and recognizable. Don't show every atom of texture or every tiny screw and nut.

- **Abstract representations** of the concept, purpose, or design principles of the product.

- **Imaginative typography** that reflects the nature of the product.

- A huge, bold **headline** with an important message.

- A short **table of contents**. As a courtesy to the reader, you may want to include a table of contents on the cover, especially if the document is a scholarly journal for readers intensely interested in the latest research findings. Be sure the table of contents is attractive and legible. Don't use this technique just to feed the vanity of authors.

- **Emblems, trademarks, or symbols** of the product.

Avoid common pitfalls

In your quest to make the cover more graphic, beware of graphics that may be confusing or misleading:

- **Unrecognizable illustrations or abstract conceptions**. One company tried generic, off-the-shelf abstract art for covers. Customers started calling the company to settle their arguments about what the cover really meant.

- **Conceptually incorrect or misleading graphics**. Don't show the top-of-the-line model if the document covers the stripped-down, economy model.

- **Graphics that are difficult or expensive to reproduce**. Continuous tone, black-and-white artwork requires halftones for proper reproduction. Color artwork requires separate printings for each color. Hairline rules may drop out when printed on inexpensive photocopy machines. No fine details show up on the computer or TV screen.

- **Graphics that are offensive or pictures that insult or patronize the reader**. Cover graphics should never belittle the reader. Although the cover designer may not intend any offense, the use of a cover that perpetuates a racial or sexual stereotype can give offense.

- **Inadvertent (or advertent) optical illusions** or graphics that produce eyestrain and discomfort in the reader. Stare at this cover for a few seconds. Notice the gray dots that flash on and off at the grid intersections.

- **Graphical fads**. Unless you are planning to replace your graphic frequently, forego the rendered 3D objects and fuzzy drop-shadows that are certain to be passé by the time this reaches print.

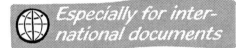

Take special care using symbolic graphics in documents for multinational or multicultural audiences. Potential problems:

☐ **Animals**. A rabbit may symbolize speed or fecundity in one country but be a dinner entrée in another and vermin in still another. Also remember that animals are often used as slurs for certain nationalities or races.

☐ **People in informal clothing**. What's cool or hip in one culture is blasphemous in another. If you must show people, show them in traditional business attire.

☐ **Abstract geometric shapes**. Especially avoid crosses, six-pointed stars, crescents, and other symbols of religious faith.

☐ **Colors**. Colors often have religious or political associations. What does orange symbolize in Northern Ireland? And red is still the color of international socialism. If you use colors, just make sure to point out their meaning and to set a context that avoids other interpretations.

Separate title and background

The title is no good if it is illegible. Avoid graphical fads, such as the current passion for using a graph-paper background to "give it a technical look." Grids can detract from legibility, especially if there is insufficient contrast between the weight, style, color, and angle of the title and that of the grid.

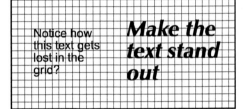

Also avoid the Web fad of using photographs for a background. See Figure 1.

Visible spine

When is a document invisible and yet in plain view? When it's wire- or comb-bound and put on the bookshelf with only the wire or comb showing. Many wire-bound documents now use a wrap-around cover to provide a surface for titles and other information.

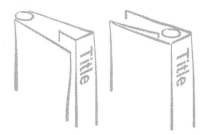

Similarly, on some comb-bound documents, the title is printed on the cylindrical comb.

Especially for electronic documents

For CD-ROM cases the spine is short and narrow. Use big letters to make the title visible. You can also add distinctive color stripes to make the spine stand out on the shelf.

Wink at the reader

OK, you've caught the reader's eye. How do you respond to invite the reader's further attention? One way is with an intriguing and meaningful title. In a glance the reader should see the rewards an acquaintance could offer.

Just for you

A clear, descriptive title identifies the intended audience. In a moment the reader can tell whether the document is for a novice, expert, or occasional user. The title also tells whether the document provides training or reference information. For example, consider each of these titles:

Figure 1: Photographic background

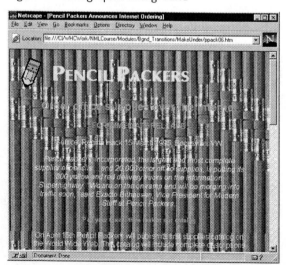

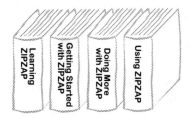

You can even use humor or wit to perk up a title.

Turning a New Leaf with XyloPage

But avoid cheeky or cutesy titles, such as these:

All You Ever Wanted to Know about ZipZap but Were Afraid to Ask

What the Heck is PROC-EXEC Anyway?

Stuff our Techno-Nerds Thought You Ought to Know

Such titles pose a special problem for those who read English as a second language-and for those who must translate documents. In such cases, avoid puns, slang, and clichés. Also, as much as you can, avoid newly minted technical terms that may be impossible to translate.

Make a promise

In the title make clear what the document offers the reader. Avoid words like *MANUAL, REGULATIONS, STANDARDS, PROCEDURES, PRELIMINARY,* and *DOCUMENTATION,* which have strongly negative connotations in the reader's mind. A title such as

DOC#46784C WRDPROC SOFTWARE PRELIMINARY REFERENCE DOCUMENTATION

not only looks foreboding but communicates little.

A better title promises the reader something in exchange. For example, these titles promise the reader successful exploration, new skills, and job satisfaction.

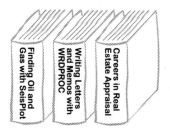

Combine title and subtitle

Try combining an intriguing title with a subtitle that elaborates and clarifies it, for example:

Zero to Web in 60 seconds

Installing and setting up your ZipWeb browser

Of course this technique only works if the subtitle appears everywhere the title does. If the title must stand alone, try reversing the technique. Combine a clear but neutral title with a snappy subtitle.

Break the ice

The reader's first attentions are tentative. You've got to work to transform curiosity into genuine interest. You've got to get acquainted and invite the reader's caresses. In other words, get the reader to browse your pages.

To invite browsing, dress in a light layout with lots of pictures, little text, and plenty of white space.

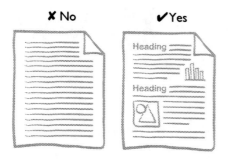

✘ No   ✔ Yes

Especially for electronic documents

For electronic documents, this technique is doubly important because users are more prone to scan than read. They bolt at the sight of an overwhelming amount of text. I once watched a usability test where users encountering a Help screen filled with text, promptly and consistently dismissed it without reading any of it. Increasingly people's expectations for electronic documents are set more by TV and videogames than by 18th century literature.

Because of glare, flicker, fingerprint smudges, and a host of other reasons, reading spans are just not as long online as on paper. You've got to make it look easy and enjoyable to consume.

3

MAKE SMALL TALK

"Hi, what's your sign?" "Nice weather we're having, eh?" "Come here often?" Small talk may not say much, but it gets a conversation going. Such opening lines build a base of common experience and trust upon which to communicate. Small talk eases the reader into the discussion. Writers call such small talk *hooks* and *leads*.

Small talk is needed wherever the reader is likely to start reading. Use a few sentences or even paragraphs of small talk at the start of the preface and introduction. Also consider using small talk at the beginning of each chapter or major section.

Before looking at all the ways to introduce a subject, let's review the things a good introduction does for the reader:

- Piques readers' interest.

- Confirms they are in the right place. If they are not, they can jump elsewhere.

- Sets expectations about the kind of information to be presented.

- Motivates them to read.

- Sets the context, if the reader jumped directly to this place in the document.

How to learn small talk

The best schools for technical small talk are the pages of popular technical and scientific magazines. Look for magazines like *Scientific American, Business Week, Popular Science,*

and others whose writers make their livings expressing complex, technical concepts in interesting and understandable prose. And while you're perusing these periodicals, read the ads. Word for word, square inch for square inch, advertisements are the most carefully crafted and most seductive of pages. Take them apart and find out what makes them seductive. Then apply these same techniques to your own documents where appropriate.

Especially for electronic documents

In electronic documents accessed by search, context sensitivity, or hypertext links, every topic is potentially Page 1 and hence could use a bit of an introduction. Yet a lengthy introduction may shove valuable content into a second scrolling zone or discourage reading altogether. Some recommendations:

- ☐ Keep the introduction short, just a sentence or two.

- ☐ Use a concise graphic that the user can take in with a glance.

- ☐ Make the topic so short and clearly organized that no introduction is needed.

Problem-solution

Begin by showing the reader a problem for which your document or product offers a solution. For example:

> An ordinary camera has its limits, as you know if you've ever dropped it on the bathroom floor, dunked it in the swimming pool, or left it to broil in your car on a summer day. But RuggedCam is no ordinary camera.

Make sure the problem is one that affects the reader and that the reader recognizes it as a problem.

"Hello, I'm ..."

One of the most honest, albeit not the most successful, techniques is to walk right up to the reader and introduce yourself, pointing out your advantages and what an acquaintance can offer.

> ZipZap PrintSerVE is a simple program that lets others on your network print on any printer attached to your computer.

First tell them **what** it is, then **why** they should care.

Name badge

In any big city, conventioneers can be identified by the plastic name badges they wear. The purpose of these badges is simply to make it easier for people to find one another and strike up conversations. The equivalent tool is the heading that clearly labels a section as a point to start reading in the document:

About this manual

What to do first

Getting started

Before you begin

What you need to get started

What is XYZ?

Why read this manual?

What you will learn

By the time readers have found the heading they want, they are ready to read. The material following the heading should get to the point right away.

Scenario

Describe a scene so that the reader can imagine it. For example:

> Outside, a chilly rain is pelting Silicon Valley on a miserable gray afternoon. Inside, comfortably ensconced in a fake living room at home–or technically, @Home–my colleague Wayt Gibbs and I are basking in the glow of a 33-inch, $5,000 Mitsubishi monitor. Officially, I have come to interview Milo Medin, @Home's vice president of networking and silicon Valley's genius of the moment. – "Do Try This @Home," *Scientific American*, January 1997.

Focus on specific objects or persons. Make the scene clear and dramatic. Include quotations if appropriate.

Definition

Begin by defining a crucial term.

> The magic square, in which every row, column and diagonal sums to the same total number, has long been a staple of recreational mathematics. – Ian Stewart, "Alphamagic Squares," *Scientific American*, January 1997.

Make the definition clear and interesting.

Question

Another way to start a conversation is to ask a provocative question and then provide the answer. For example:

> The hard part of an expedition to Mars isn't getting there, but coming back. More than three-fourths of what is launched to Mars is the return vehicle, supporting equipment, and fuel: 136 metric tons to return a crew of four.
>
> So why bring them back?
>
> – Henry Spencer, "One-Way to Mars?", *Wired*, January, 1997.

Or show how a new technology raises multiple questions–which you offer to answer.

> An Intel spokesman recently estimated that 80 percent of PCs would have 3D graphics capability by 2000. What should we do with this enormous increase in the availability of computer graphics? What tools and applications will we need? How will we address the concurrent growth in the visualization of non scientific data, and how will burgeoning areas such as the World Wide Web be affected by the wide availability of 3D computer graphics? The Technical Committee on Computer Graphics seeks to answer these important questions and many other through its conferences, symposia, workshops, and publications. – "Computer Graphics Technical Committee," *Computer*, November 1996.

Curiosity is a powerful motivator. Unleash it with questions.

Technical breakthrough

Start by giving the reader a glimpse of a significant technical advance. Tell how the subject is an improvement compared to others of its type:

> Prospecting for oil and gas used to be a matter of simply looking for places where oil seeps to the surface, drilling nearby and hoping for the best. These days the search for civilization's lifeblood is more scientific, and oil companies spend many millions of dollars studying the types of rock formations most likely to have trapped worthwhile reserves. Now they have a new tool that could help find places worth exploring–and so eliminate some expensive dry holes. – "More Gallons per Mile," Scientific American, January 1997.

The breakthrough does not have to be world-shaking, merely important to the reader.

Contrast

Begin with a startling contrast. You could, for instance, contrast then and now, revealing deterioration or improvement:

> There was a time, not long ago, when a sophisticated research strategy involved traveling downtown to the main library; consulting with the reference librarian; and spending hours poring over the card catalog, the *Reader's Guide* and finally the dusty stacks of books and magazines.

> Well, sweep the dust away and power up the computer: "sophisticated" has taken on new meaning with the advent of searchable computer databases that are affordable and easily accessible using a personal computer and CompuServe. — Cathryn Conroy, "Search Strategies," *Online Today*, July 1987.

Or you could contrast appearances and reality by showing the difference between what seems to be true to the reader and what really is true:

> For years, motivational speakers have celebrated the Yale study on why people succeed. It's powerful! Compelling! Too bad it doesn't exist. – Lawrence Tabak, "If Your Goal is Success, Don't Consult These Gurus," *Fast Company*, January 1997.

In sales documents you may want to contrast *them* and *you*. Show the reader the difference between the product you are describing and a competing one. Of course, your product comes out ahead in the comparison:

> Most premium cassettes are designed to perform well enough at room temperature and moderate humidity. At TDK, we know our cassettes will often be used in less than ideal conditions and we're not satisfied until we know our tape and our mechanism will perform in almost any environment they might encounter. — TDK advertisement

Shocker or tickler

Give the reader some startling or intriguing fact or statistic about the subject:

> Every day Americans throw away the staggering total of 800 million pounds of trash. — U. S. Steel ad, *Omni,* October 1979.

Or just say something provocative.

> "Stop for lunch and you are lunch." It's the latest Silicon Valley sound bite—a reminder of the insatiable competitive appetite, the technological hunger, the financial thirst that gnaws in the bellies of California's ravenous business hyperachievers.— "Report from the Future," *Fast Company*, January 1997.

Though you want to surprise or perhaps challenge the reader, take care not to insult the reader.

Funnel in

To introduce an esoteric subject start with a broad statement the reader is sure to understand and agree with. Then present narrower and narrower statements to focus the reader's thoughts on the main idea of the piece.

> Designing a new house is a complex activity. Plans must be drawn, construction activities spelled out, and required components listed. The number of such components may extend to the thousands. Keeping track of them requires a database like BuildeRBase by Structware.

Visually the structure resembles a funnel, broad at the top and narrow at the bottom.

Such a structure is especially useful in electronic documents where the reader can jump to this topic from almost anywhere. The funnel provides a smooth transition and context for the tightly focused content.

Picture this

Provide an overview graphic to plant the right mental model of a process or procedure or a set of interrelated components. Or a picture of potential results à la cookbooks. Such graphical tables of contents or menus are especially important in electronic documents where they can suggest the structure of topics the user must navigate to learn further details.

First person, first interest

Tell the reader how you got interested in a subject, how an important question occurred to you, or how you made a revealing discovery.

> I first met Betty, a blind teenager in Toronto, as I was interviewing participants for an upcoming study of mine on touch perception in 1973. Betty had lost her sight at age two, when she was too young to have learned to draw. So I was astonished when she told me that she liked to draw profiles of her family members. Before I began working with the blind, I had always thought of pictures as copies of the visible world. — John M. Kennedy, "How the Blind Draw", *Scientific American*, January 1997.

Pick incidents that will produce the same results in your reader's imagination as in your real experience.

Quotation

Begin with a succinct, surprising quotation, perhaps from a satisfied customer.

> "It even saved the groceries."

> "All right, we did lose one egg," admit both Patricia and Robert Steves. But considering the accident they were involved in, they don't seem to mind. — Ad for Saturn cars.

You can also use a literary quotation, provided its meaning is relevant or ironic.

Warm-up act

With multimedia, words can speak for themselves and pictures can move. Thus we can create more compelling, more informative, and more entertaining introductions. Some ideas:

- Animation showing an overview of a dynamic process or procedure.
- Video of a recognized authority explaining why the material is important.
- Musical fanfare.

Just don't overdo it. Try it out on some test readers first.

Document halitosis

Some forms of small talk, however, can be offensive to readers.

- A patronizing or condescending tone. "You may not know it but ...."
- Overdone congratulations on having the wisdom, the sagacity, the absolute brilliance to buy the product. "You are one smart buyer!"
- Forcing the user to memorize arcane and abstruse terminology.

Editor's tip #1

If you do not have time to rewrite the entire document, have a rewrite specialist add introductions to already written material.

Editor's tip #2

Also, do not try to write introductions in the first draft. Get the content right, then add introductions. Otherwise how to do you know what you are introducing?

KEEP THE CONVERSATION GOING

Unity. Oneness. Coherence. Without them any piece of writing falls to pieces. Smooth talking can smooth the way, but there are no gimmicks to conceal or patch up a lack of unity. Linking devices can only reveal the inherent coherence of your writing. Without a clear plan derived from a definite purpose, your writing will never have the underlying organization that provides this unity. So organize, write, and then use the techniques that follow to string the pieces more tightly together.

Especially for electronic documents

In applying the techniques of this section, keep in mind that users seldom read long passages of electronic documents. In fact, well designed electronic documents get right to the point without requiring lengthy reading. Users who access electronic documents by hypertext links, context sensitivity, and search mechanisms view topics in an order the author cannot predict.

For these reasons, we must apply the following techniques to promote consistency between topics and continuity within topics.

Echo

Repeat an idea in different words. Start a new paragraph with a word or phrase that summarizes or at least refers to a major segment of the preceding paragraph.

> What happens if you get sick or go on vacation? Your work area must continue to operate, even if you're not there; someone has to take your place and do the kind of tasks you do each day.
>
> That's why it's a good idea for you to have a backup system administrator who can fill in for you.
> — "Having a Backup Administrator," *Planning for Your System: Virtual Machine/Integrated System,* IBM Corporation.

Visually we can represent this transition like this:

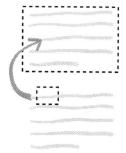

A variation of this technique is to use a term at the end of one paragraph and then define it at the beginning of the next paragraph. The natural tension pulls the reader into the next paragraph. The technique succeeds, however, only if the definition is provided.

To link to information on the World Wide Web you use a *uniform resource locator* or URL for short.

The URL is a concise set of instructions for finding an individual piece of information. Go to this server, look in that directory in a certain subdirectory at a particular location in a specific file.

This structure reverses that of the first example. Here the second paragraph expands the small item at the end of the first.

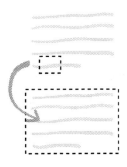

Linking words and phrases

The English language is rich with words and phrases whose sole purpose is to tie two ideas together while revealing the relationship between them. Table 1 lists such terms.

Repeated key word or object

Repeat an especially important word or phrase. Begin a paragraph by repeating a term or phrase from the last sentence of the preceding paragraph.

Table 1: Linking words and phrases

Add	Compare	Contrast	Specify	Sequence	Refer back	Show result
more	likewise	however	one such	now	the above	thus
moreover	in like man-	nevertheless	for instance	then	this	so
in addition	ner	but	for example	after	that	therefore
and	similarly	yet	one, two,	before	such	hence
more impor-	here again	though	three, ...	already	(any summa-	accordingly
tant		although	in fact	so far	rizing pro-	consequently
another		even though	such	recently	noun)	because
note that		otherwise	in particular	more recently		of course
also		conversely	first, second,	lately		presumably
too			third ...	finally		evidently
in fact				at last		
furthermore				meanwhile		
besides				later		
yet				formerly		
another				subsequently		

Investigators took handwriting samples, fingerprints, and clippings of hair from each of the suspects. That evening they drove the hair samples the 350 kilometers to the Provincial forensic laboratory for DNA analysis.

DNA provided the key to understanding the crime and eventually nabbing the murderer.

Here, a word or phrase at the start of a paragraph hooks onto the same word or phrase at the end of the preceding paragraph.

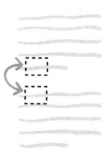

Or begin each of a series of paragraphs with the same words, much like the kind of litany found in religious ceremonies from Rome to Katmandu.

> The Global Navigation System, GloNav for short, provides ...
>
> GloNav saves ...
>
> GloNav simplifies ...
>
> GloNav prevents...
>
> GloNav eliminates ...

This technique returns attention to the subject of the overall section at the beginning of each new paragraph. It works best when the paragraphs are a few sentences long. It can seem monotonous in a series of one-sentence paragraphs, and the parallelism gets lost if the paragraphs are spread out over several pages.

You can also apply this technique graphically. Start with a graphical overview

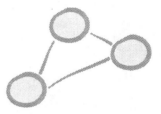

Then, as you discuss each object in the graphic, begin by showing an enlargement of the object under discussion.

Or repeat the overview graphic but with the object under discussion highlighted.

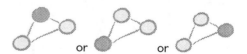

In an electronic document, make the overview graphic a menu so the user can click on a part of the overview to jump to the discussion of that part.

Consistent viewpoint

Often you can smooth the flow of your writing by maintaining a consistent viewpoint and expressing it by repeating grammatical patterns.

> ... we had no electric power. ... Our studies showed .... We decided to .... We next had to decide on .... We arrived at the following .... we wanted .... we used .... we have .... — Bernard Cain, "Wind-Powered Bubbler," *Popular Science,* December 1979.

The pattern can be blatant or it can be subtle.

Road map and signposts

Tell the reader where you are going and what signposts mark the way. Signposts are key phrases, proper nouns, numbers (first, second, third, ...) that identify the parts of the subject. Don't forget to erect the signposts.

> The display is divided into two columns. On the left is the overview list and on the right the detailed view.

> The overview list ...

> The detailed view ...

The signposts can take the form of words in text, headings, icons, or graphics.

Psychological momentum

To avoid throwing the reader for a loop, move in a direction the reader can predict. Some common directional conventions are:

- Cause to effect
- Past to future
- Abstract to concrete
- Specific to general
- Familiar to unfamiliar

After a general accusation, **we expect** specific facts to back up the charge. After a detailed case study, **we expect** the writer to generalize the specific facts so we can see how they apply to us.

Elbow joint

Plumbers use elbow joints to change direction in which liquid flows. Writers use elbow joints to direct the reader's thoughts in a new direction.

> The end came suddenly, and from an unlikely competitor.

> The product that ultimately doomed CompCal was not one of its more advanced competitors, but a simple machine that had been around for 50 years.

It was the "statistical permutator," a contraption of brass gears and rosewood case.

Visually you can think of this transition like this:

It clearly signals the reader that you are diverting from the expected direction.

Sudden reversal

As strange as it may seem, the sudden reversal can be a transitional device, for example:

> At last the American space program seemed back on track.
>
> Until three months later when the Vanguard rocket rose three feet into the air before settling back onto its launch pad in an explosion of flame and disappointment.

The trick is to make the reversal clear—and a bit ironical. This technique works especially well for jumping from one paragraph to another.

Clear structure

Of course, some pieces do not need explicit transitions or linking devices. Examples are catalog entries and pieces written in outline form. Their basic organization provides the needed structural unity. Reference documents are often accessed by reading headings to narrow in on a topic. Such documents are searched hierarchically instead of sequentially. These documents exhibit a clear and logical structure. To make the structure apparent, use one of these techniques:

Checklist for revealing structure

☐ Incorporate a table of contents to show the overall structure.

☐ Index topics so the reader can jump directly to the appropriate part of the document.

☐ Number the steps of a procedure.

☐ Put alternatives in bulleted lists.

☐ Make headings and other targets of scanning distinct from text. Set them in a larger or bolder typeface.

☐ Number headings.

☐ Indent subordinate material.

☐ Emphasize especially important material by boxing it or surrounding it with blank space.

Blaze a trail for the user

Make it as easy to "flip the pages" in electronic documents as in paper ones. Provide Next and Previous buttons the user can click to follow a trail. Such trails are sometimes called browse sequences or tours.

Where should the trail go? Assume you have a document organized into a hierarchy of topics like this:

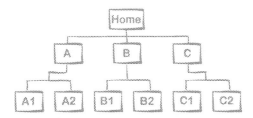

You can pick from three main strategies:

- **Depth-first**. (Home, A, A1, A2, B, B1, B2, C, C1, C2). This pathway mimics the sequence of pages in a technical manual. It is good for users who want to read the whole document in detail.

- **Siblings-first**. (Home, A, B, C, A1, A2, B1, B2, C1, C2). This pathway gives a complete overview at a level before diving down to the next level of detail.

- **Ad hoc**. (You decide). You designate a sequence of topics to fit a special purpose. The path may pass through all topics or only a few especially important ones. This is a way you can add value by revealing what you know readers really need to know.

5

NOT
GOODBYE BUT
AU REVOIR

Parting is sweet sorrow when we know the beloved will return. To ensure the beloved reader returns, we end the piece with what journalists call a *twist*.

The way you end the piece depends on what you want the reader to do. You may just want the reader to nod approvingly at the ideas presented. You may want the reader to take further action after putting down the document. You may want the reader to take up arms in your cause. You *never* want to leave the reader hanging, uncertain whether the writing has ended.

So how do we end a seductive document or passage?

Summarize

One of the most common endings is a quick review of the main points.

> In short, the high storage capacity, low duplication costs, and remarkable durability make CD-ROM ideal for distributing census data.

If there are more than a few points, make them a list: a bullet list for choices, a checklist for requirements, or a numbered list for steps to take or rankings. Let the user tear out or print out the summary.

Recall main advantage

A reminder of your product's best feature leaves the reader with a good taste.

> There are a lot of underwater cameras on the market but none go to greater depths to deliver great pictures than AquaCam.

Tell the reader to act

If you've stated your case convincingly, then it's time readers get off their duffs and do something. Tell them to get moving.

> For more information about ZipZap, enter GO ZIPZAP at the main menu and then select MORE INFO from the ZipZap menu.

Sometimes you have to be bossy to propel a passive reader into action. If you feel uneasy about ordering your readers around, provide the information readers need to act and leave them to decide whether to act.

> This new communications service is being tested by cable TV providers in Orlando, San Jose, and Vancouver now. If all goes well, you'll be able to order it from your cable company later this year. For more information, call TVConGa at 1-800-555-1234.

Make sure to provide enough information for the user to act: phone numbers, addresses, e-mail addresses, Web addresses, part numbers, and so forth.

Make the reader think and feel

If you can't make your readers act, at least make them think about what you have said.

> Picture yourself using the most accurate voltmeter in the world. Now what can't you do?

Sometimes you want the reader to think about the consequences of ignoring your advice.

> Of course you may feel that documenting your decisions takes too much time. Until you have to explain to an auditor the basis for your decisions.

For this technique to succeed it must trigger the correct emotion: pleasure, fear, confidence.

Point forward

As you conclude, propel the reader onward toward new ideas.

> Over the next few months you'll see big improvements throughout this Web site—richer content, easier access, and eye-popping displays. Did we mention the games? See you here.

You can suggest an application of the idea or product you have covered. You can cite a new problem or future benefit for it. Give the reader a feeling of positive motion.

Funnel out

To prevent the reader from saying "so what" at the end of the passage, include a few statements showing the broader implications of what you have said.

> Right now trinary tunneling protocol lives in only a handful of experimental projects in university laboratories. Yet in a few years it could power corporate data networks, the World Wide Web, and even cable TV systems.

The funnel out has the opposite structure as the funnel in technique used for an introduction.

In many ways it is like the cinematic technique of zooming back from a tight close-up in order to show surrounding objects and provide context.

Wave goodbye

Headings are often used to label points of departure in technical documents.

Practice

For more information

Review

Summary

Where to go from here

On your own

Such headings forewarn the reader that the end is near. If readers know that a section is the last in a series, its end does not seem abrupt or arbitrary.

Test, err I mean, game

Give readers an opportunity to apply what they have learned. Doing so locks in the information or skills they have learned and gives them a chance to correct any misinterpretations they have formed. The traditional way is to test the reader. Alas "test" is one of the least seductive words invented. Instead, call it an "activity" or "game." Figure 2 shows an example of a quiz from a computer-based training lesson. It looks like a jig-saw puzzle. It works like a jig-saw puzzle. It's just as much fun.

Figure 2: Game used as a test

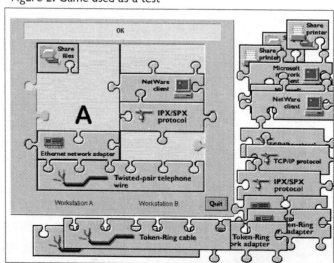

6

GET AND STAY IN SHAPE

Trim and fit are *de rigueur* today. Documents must shed those unnecessary pages of flab and replace them with muscular content that sleekly and efficiently delivers information.

Put the document on a diet

From all sides the citizen reader is over-loaded with information. Consider these facts:

- Over 5,500 medical papers are pub-lished each day.

- Each year the U.S. Congress passes 500 laws, and regulatory agencies issue 10,000 regulations. State legislatures pass another 25,000 laws.

- In the Pentagon, 350,000 photocopies are made each day.

- The average American family watches over 51 hours of television a week, or more than 7 hours a day.

Yet, consider the length of these influential and not so influential documents:

Lord's Prayer	56 words
Gettysburg Address	266 words
Ten Commandments	297 words
Declaration of Inde-pendence	300 words
Box of breakfast cereal	1,200 words
U.S. Government order on pricing cabbage	26,911 words

Perhaps Carlyle's injunction on litera-ture applies to technical writing as well:

"There is a great discovery still to be made in Literature, that of paying lit-erary men by the quantity they do not write. "

— Thomas Carlyle

Writers of business and technical documents must confront the infamous Curve of Di-minishing Readership.

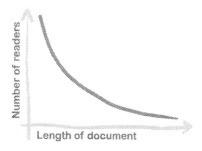

We more readily read a pamphlet than a tome. We consume more magazines than books. Thin brochures get more readers than obese documents. The smaller docu-ments require less immediate commitment, effort, and obligation from the reader.

The probability of someone reading something is inversely proportional to the cube of its length.
— "Horton's Laws." R. John Brockmann and William Horton, *The Writer's Pocket Almanack.*

Formal research studies and informal usability tests alike have found that users avoid large, complex documents because using them "looks like too much work."

These users realize the basic axiom,

> Time spent reading the manual is not spent doing the job.

So, let's design leaner, more athletic documents.

Cull and winnow

Looking for a needle in the proverbial haystack is no easy matter, but it is considerably easier if the haystack is a small one. Anything we can do to narrow the reader's field of search will reduce the time required to find the necessary information. The reader will not only find information more quickly, but will also more likely try in the first place.

The writer must beware of what *Byte* magazine editor Chris Morgan has called the "penguin syndrome" after a letter received a few years ago by a publisher of children's books. The letter, in a child's scrawl, offered these words:

> Dear Sirs: I am returning your book because it told me more about penguins than I wanted to know.

Keep in mind that often your task is not to tell readers everything.

✗ No	✔ Yes
Every way to do everything.	The best way to do the most common things.

One of the most important duties of an editor is to delete unnecessary information. If not removed, such information obscures needed information, bores some readers, and frightens others. If in doubt, leave it out.

> I believe more in the scissors than I do in the pencil.
>
> — Truman Capote

Remember the classic 80-20 rule: 80% of the work can be done with 20% of the information. Find that 20% and you can probably delete the other 80% to good effect.

Remember, it does no good to answer a question that no one asks. Successful deleting takes more than an ample supply of blue pencils—it takes lots of testing. By testing prototypes of the document with actual users in realistic situations, we can better gauge whether information is necessary or whether it is supplied by the context of the task at hand or by the user's background experience.

Lean documents

Let users write the document. To create a concise but effective document, use our exclusive no-cost usability testing method.

Ingredients

Two users (or reasonable surrogates)

Observer (that's you)

Video camera or tape recorder (These are optional. If the users object to being taped, just take notes).

Expert (someone who knows the product, technology, or system you are writing about)

Prototype of the product (If a prototype is not available, have a subject-matter expert simulate the product.)

Realistic task for the users to perform

Procedure

Give the users a task to perform, but **no documentation or training**. Tell them if they have questions they can ask them of the expert. Also explain that they do not have to ask questions. They can figure things out on their own if they prefer. They can experiment with the prototype. They can meditate and wait for psychic inspiration for all you care.

The expert can answer their questions but cannot volunteer information. The answers do not have to be "yes" or "no." Answers can be complete explanations. The expert can answer in words, draw pictures, and demonstrate actions. The one thing the subject-matter expert should not do is to volunteer information the users have not asked for. This means that you, the observer, must intervene if the expert tries to help the users without being asked or if you feel the answer to a question strays beyond the scope of the question.

Here's the basic cycle:

1.   The users try to do a step. If they get stuck they ask a question.
2.   The expert answers the question.
3.   You prompt the users to paraphrase the answer.
4.   If the expert agrees that the paraphrase is essentially correct.
     A.   You write down the paraphrase.
     B.   The users perform the step and continue the process

At the end of the test, you string together the paraphrases and you have a concise first draft.

Now repeat the test with another two test subjects. But this time, give the test subjects the first draft you derived from the first test. If the first draft is not sufficient, that is, if the new users have additional questions, add the answers to the draft before the next text. After a few rounds of testing you have a draft that is written in the user's terms and concepts, expressed at their level of experience, containing just what they needed to know with nothing wasted.

Visit users and take notes

Visit users where they work. Observe summaries they have created for themselves:

- Notes thumbtacked to the wall, stuck to the edge of the computer screen, or taped onto the keyboard

- Notebooks of information they keep at hand

- Things they have underlined, highlighted, or bookmarked in the manual

- Annotations and bookmarks in Help files, Web pages, and other electronic documents

If something was important enough for a user to write it down, it is important enough to go in your document.

Summarize

Every big book needs a little companion. If you must produce a big book for contractual requirements or just to record all the facts, then include a condensed summary. Boil the large mass of information down to its essential points.

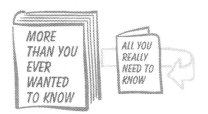

Such summaries take many forms:

- Concise handbook, pamphlet, or booklet

- Reference card for pocket or keyboard

- Wall chart or poster

- Foldout page

In electronic documents provide a special quick-reference summary topic that users can print out.

Caution: once the pamphlet is available, don't plan on selling too many of the big books.

Customize

Not all users need all the information all the time. But writers of big, general-purpose documents often assume everyone needs to know everything. We must realize that, with the possible exceptions of the Mercury space capsule and the White House hotline, technological products are not used by just one person for one purpose under one set of circumstances. Most products are used by a variety of users for an assortment of tasks under widely varying conditions.

One way to give users less to read is to create a series of small documents, each designed to guide one type of user in performing one kind of task. For instance, consider a computer system. Typically one person purchases it, another installs and services it, another operates it, and still another may program special functions for it. Each person performs a different task requiring different information. Each needs a separate document, customized to the task.

Who Needs what information	Installation	Advantages	Programming	Operating	Startup	Repair
Operator				✓	✓	
Buyer		✓				
Programmer			✓	✓	✓	
Repairman	✓			✓	✓	✓

Next, replace the check marks with more detailed notes on the type of document to use for each purpose: brochure, pamphlet, Help file, Web page, and so forth.

You may chose to consolidate similar needs to reduce the number of separate docu-ments you must produce. You may, for example, group together into one docu-ment different kinds of information needed by a single reader.

Though we can't often write individual in-structions for each separate user, we can at least identify the groups using the product and give each group just the information it needs—and nothing more. We can publish a series of small instruction documents rather than one all-inclusive tome. We can use word-processing and database systems to custom-tailor the documents for specialized groups of users. See Figure 3.

Or we can publish on index cards or loose-leaf pages and encourage users to select and arrange the pieces to suit their needs.

Figure 3: Using a database to custom-tailor manuals

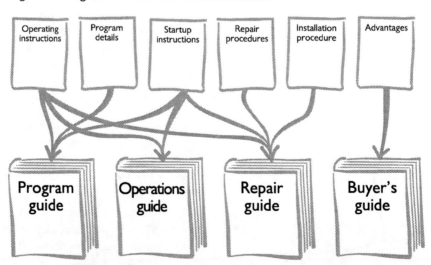

Dress to look thinner

Perceived size sometimes differs from physical reality. Size is often subjective and is affected by expectations, appetite, and first impressions. For this reason, don't put a 27-page document in an 8-1/2 x 11-inch binder with a 3-inch spine.

Paragraphs on the screen seem longer than on paper. Download time seems longer than it really is.

On the other hand, need, interest, and curiosity can make a lengthy document seem petite and nimble. If the document exactly covers the reader's need (and the reader realizes this), then the document is exactly the right size, whether it is 6 or 6000 pages.

Cure anorexic documents

In general, smaller documents are more likely to be read. But are some documents too thin? Are there anorexic documents? Is minimalism minimizing your readership?

Yes. It is easy to produce a small document by simply leaving out enough information. Symptomatic of anorexic documentation is the spate of third-party books that appear after a product is shipped with just a pamphlet-sized manual.

An incomplete Help system is often self-defeating. Users quickly learn they cannot depend on Help to answer all their questions and stop using it.

I try to leave out the parts that people skip.

— Elmore Leonard

We might add, "... and only the parts people skip."

One problem with especially small documents is that they have bad bookshelf manners. They squirm and flop and slither inside or behind their co-residents on the bookcase. Further complicating matters is the fact that small documents often lack a spine. The result is that the reader can't find small documents, even when they are within easy reach.

Layer information

If we cannot write a smaller book, we can at least ensure that the reader has to read less of it. All books contain various general types or levels of information. Information can be presented at various levels of abstraction, levels of detail, levels of generality, and levels of applicability. We must then enable the reader to navigate the document, selecting the proper level for the purpose at hand.

For instance, a novice needs detailed instructions on how to get started using the product, while an expert needs only general guidelines and operating principles. An experienced but infrequent user may need just a reminder of specific details.

The strategy of the writer should be to let the reader quickly find the appropriate level. To do this we must:

- Group the information into layers.
- Clearly distinguish each layer.
- Enable the reader to move among layers.

The writer must anticipate the sequence of questions that the reader asks when confronted with the document. Is this the correct document? What kinds of information does it contain? What kinds do I need? How is it structured? How do I find the information I need?

Try these techniques for organizing multi-level documents in the following checklist.

Organizing multi-level documents

- ☐ Print different types of information in different colors of ink or on different colors of paper.

- ☐ Precede each major section with a brief overview.

- ☐ Include a table of contents for each section.

- ☐ Provide maps and other visual indicators of the sequence and hierarchy of the document.

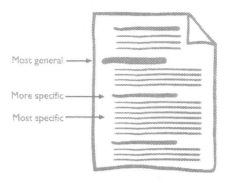

- ☐ Vary indentation, type size, weight, font, line spacing, and other typographic details to indicate different levels.

In electronic documents layering is easier and often more effective. Deeper layers are never in the way and almost endless reserves of information are possible. But to apply layering online, we have to take a more sophisticated view of layering. In electronic documents, layering just refers to the degree of difficulty of finding accessing information. Shallow layers are those the user can get to with a minimum of thought and effort. They require just a few button clicks. The user can jump to them directly from the main menu or Home page. They can be retrieved with simple single-word queries. To get to deeper layers, users must click the mouse more, follow a longer trail of hypertext links, or type in a complex query full of ANDs, ORs, and NOTs.

Use shallow layers for information that is ...	Use deeper layers for information that is ...
Critical	Nice to know
Needed by many	Needed by few
Immediately useful	Theoretical background

Design the body for fast scanning

Consumers of technical documents differ from readers of novels in that they do not so much read as search for a nugget of information. They skim. They skip. They scan. While searching, they are completely unconcerned with the rest of the text. In fact, the better it stays out of the way, the more likely they are to find the information they seek.

To assist the scanning reader, we must design the document not so much for reading word by word from cover to cover, but for quick and efficient skimming at maximum speed. While skimming, the reader is not trying to absorb the information flying by but rather merely trying to spot and recognize the facts needed. Our goal is to reveal general content and significance of the words without forcing the reader actually read them.

Make headings meaningful

Headings are signposts. They alert the skimming reader to upcoming attractions, perilous twists, tricky turns, and time-consuming detours. Properly designed headings allow the skimmer to traverse the document at high speed without losing a bird's-eye view of the terrain below.

To keep the skimmer informed, we should use *active* headings instead of passive labels. Active headings communicate. They are not merely cryptic mileposts ticking off the pages. They say exactly what the document contains. Active headings include:

- Questions: **What is CAISP?**
- Complete sentences: **CAISP teaches spelling.**
- Ellipses: **To start CAISP ...**

Active headings give the fast-skimming reader useful information as well as a clear sense of what the accompanying text contains.

Especially for electronic documents

Readers of electronic documents often access information by selecting from a list of titles of topics. Typically third-order headings in paper documents become the titles of third-level topics in electronic documents. If you are authoring a paper document that has an electronic version in its future, review your headings to make sure they will work as titles. And if lots of users will print out sequences of topics from your electronic document, make sure the titles work as headings.

Web pages and other electronic documents demand more of titles than do paper documents. Often the user must select from a list of titles proffered by the system. Titles for electronic documents must be:

☐ **Meaningful out of context**. If the only way to understand the title is to read the content, most readers will just skip over it. Watch out for titles that are clever puns or that rely on the first lines of text or a graphic to reveal their full meaning.

☐ **Predictive**. Users should be able to guess what they will receive in reward for clicking on a title's button.

☐ **Front loaded**. Users should be able to scan down a list of titles and quickly find the one they want. In a simple vertical scan the eye can take in only two or three words. So put the most critical words up front. Doing so avoids the problem that occurs when the ends of titles are cut off when they appear in a narrow window.

Come to think of it, these are not bad ideas for paper documents too.

Spell out who does what

For multiperson procedures, we can use a special form of headings called *playscript*. Playscript resembles the script for a Broadway play, except that the actors are the participants in the procedure and instead of dialogue the playscript tells them what actions to take. For example:

Mechanic	Open hood and inspect engine.
Driver	Crank engine.
Mechanic	Check for sounds of air leaks in hoses.
Driver	Race engine two or three times.
Mechanic	Listen for backfiring.

This format is versatile. The "actors" do not have to be persons. They can be teams. Or one can be a person and another a machine, for example, when explaining how a machine responds to inputs from a user. Or both can be machines if explaining how two machines interact.

Use typography for topography

There's nothing more boring than flying over endless prairie. The eye longs for some three-dimensional relief. We pine to see a mountain range or at least a few foothills. The same is true when flying over a document. In a document we can use typography, or choice of type, to separate the high ground from the valleys and plains. We can use:

- Type font (Times Roman, `Courier`, **Helvetica**).
- Type style (regular, **bold**, *italic*).
- Type size (Headline, 12-point, `10-pitch`, agate).
- Underlining.
- CAPITALIZATION.
- Color

Use these factors to make headings stand out from body text and to distinguish one level of heading from another. As rule ensure a 30 to 60 percent difference in prominence between levels and between the lowest level and body text. The difference can come from a combination of factors, say size, color, and boldness.

Not only can we use typography to make the headings more legible and emphatic; but we can also use it to clearly distinguish warnings, cautions, notes, examples, key terms, and important concepts.

Lay out for fast scanning

The way words and pictures are configured on the page can help or hinder scanning. For fastest scanning, lay out information in multiple columns. To make headings stand out, put them in one column and the text in another. This will also keep both headings and lines of text short enough to be read without sideways movement of the vertically scanning eyes. You can even use a third column for illustrations and notes.

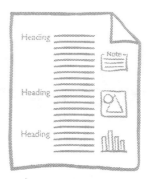

By putting the text in a column by itself, you prevent unnecessary interruptions by illustrations, tables, headings, and notes. This layout also lets you place illustrations and tables near related text.

Use you-are-here headers and footers

Have you ever been driving along a stretch of freeway late at night, perhaps listening to some late-night talk show on the radio, and suddenly realized you had driven past your exit? That's the feeling that scanners of technical documents often get if you don't take pains to give them you-are-here maps like those found in shopping centers and large office buildings. We can put this kind of navigational aid in the top and bottom margins of the document. Include such things as chapter number and title, page number, and topic being discussed. You may also want to include date or version of the publication.

For electronic documents, you can show the path from the top menu or Home page to the current topic. Figure 4 shows an example.

Design for efficient lookup

Reading and scanning both employ *sequential access*. In this type of access, the reader proceeds more or less sequentially through the document from the beginning until he finds what he is looking for or gives up.

But there is another way of seeking information, called *random access.* In random access the reader does not peruse the document but directly seeks out the single table, paragraph, or illustration needed. Random access is nothing exotic. We use it every time we look up a word in the dictionary or consult an encyclopedia. If you kept a record of the pages you used in your dictionary, you would discover a nearly random pattern.

Hence the name, *random access.*

But your lookup searching is far from random. It is as systematic as possible. The material is organized in such a way that you can go right to the single piece of information you need without having to read or even scan anything else.

In designing a document for efficient random access, it is not enough to clearly present the information. We must also label that information to make it instantly accessible. Some aids to the user are the table of contents, index, and tabs.

Use table of contents to show structure

The table of contents shows what the document contains and how it is organized. To provide this overview, format the contents so that the reader can see the overall plan in a single glance. This means that the

Figure 4: Location indicators

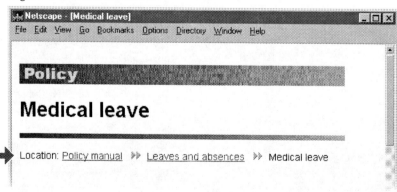

table of contents should be no longer than a page or, at most, two facing pages. Include two or three levels of headings, not more. If you need to give more details, you can always include a second, more detailed table of contents. Or, better still, you can put a detailed table of contents at the start of each chapter or major section.

Many electronic documents include an expanding outline that both shows the organization of the document and provides one-click access to individual topics. See Figure 5.

Include a task-specific index

An index helps the user find specific facts. No document over a few pages should be without one. A useful index anticipates what the user will look for and includes these topics in terms the user can understand. An index that merely lists system nomenclature (IEBGENR, IEEE401.C, object dispatcher) is next to useless to an uninitiated user trying to perform a simple task such as printing a memo. Instead, the index should list tasks the user will want to perform (how to get started, how to enter text, how to print out text, how to quit). See Figure 6 to compare a feature-only index to one including tasks.

Figure 5: Using a table of contents to show structure

Especially for electronic documents

For electronic documents, the index contains hypertext links rather than page numbers. This way the user merely clicks on the index entry to jump to the topic it refers to. Do you see a problem? Paper indexes can refer to multiple pages for a single entry. But a hypertext link can only jump to one destination. This means that online indexes must be more specific than those on paper. The online index presents an additional level of choices, either indented under the primary choice or displayed in a window that pops up after the primary choice is selected.

Paper index

Copying files, 35, 38, 72

Electronic index

Copying files
    Drag and drop
    Menu command
    Copy command

Use tabs to label major sections

Tab pages divide a menacingly large book into less threatening chunks. Good tabs don't merely list the chapter number. They use terms the reader can easily recognize and fully understand. Or they forego words altogether and use simple visual symbols.

Figure 6: Comparison of two indexes

Feature-only index

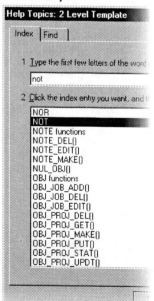

Task-and feature index

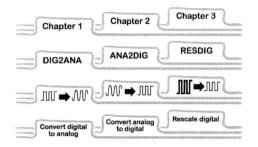

Tabs are expensive. If you cannot afford true tabs, use bleed tabs instead. Bleed tabs imprint the tab label on a bar of color that extends to the to the outside edge of the page. When the pages are fanned, the bars of color are visible to the reader.

Tabs are also a popular metaphor in electronic documents. Though often misused, this metaphor works for people who are accustomed to finding this information on paper in filing cabinets. See Figure 7.

Figure 7: Filing cabinet metaphor

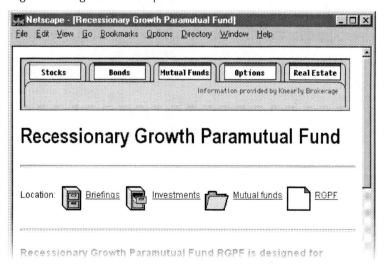

7

PRACTICE HEROIC HEDONISM

Seduction promises pleasure. But a puritanical ethic often blocks writers. They have correctly observed that interesting documents are often shallow and inaccurate. Such drivel and marketing fluff give seduction a bad name and lead many writers to employ a bare and stark presentation that they believe to be more technically honest. If it doesn't taste bad, it isn't medicine. If it isn't dull, it isn't technical.

But hedonism can have a place. We can deliver pleasure and keep our integrity at the same time. Techniques include:

- Interesting style.
- Pleasing graphic design.
- Appropriate humor.

Offer psychological rewards

The best ways of delivering pleasure, the most heroic forms of hedonism, are psychological. We must give the user a feeling of achievement and fulfillment. The document must give positive and encouraging feedback.

> You've now completed lesson 3. Congratulations. You've covered some difficult material and have now mastered the three main elements of using SeisPlot. You can now begin using it to make simple maps and charts of your own exploration data.

Remember that most people respond to success and praise better than to failure and criticism. Words are not enough. We must reward with the satisfaction that results from successfully demonstrating new skills or applying new knowledge.

Make the reader laugh

Humor can relax the reader and create a mood receptive to your message. Sources of humor include:

- Cartoons, such as a continuing cartoon character who points out important information and warns about potential pitfalls.

- Old photographs, line drawings, etchings, and other artwork with an ironical connection to the subject.

Optional equipment?

- Quotations appropriate or ironical in context.

The book *An Introduction to Operating Systems* began the chapter on file and database systems with this quotation:

> Remember thee!
> Ay, thou poor ghost, while *memory* holds a seat
> In this distracted globe. Remember thee!
> Yea, from the *table* of my *memory*
> I'll wipe away all trivial fond *records*,
> All saws of books, all *forms*, all pressures past,
> That youth and observation *copied* there. — William Shakespeare, *Hamlet*, I:v:95.

The words in italics are also technical terms that describe parts and actions of a database system.

The key is subtlety: whimsical rather than ribald humor.

No jests are so insipid as those which parade the fact that they are intended to be witty.
— Quintillian

If you use humor, never belittle the user or (if you value your paycheck) your employer's product. Especially avoid puns, which writers tend to like more than the general populace and which baffle most people whose first language is not English. Avoid humor in documents intended for a multinational or multicultural audience. Humor, even effective humor, is almost impossible to translate.

Please leave the bad jokes for your next cocktail party and only tell me how to do it.
— Joanne Groshardt

If you have any doubts about your skill as a comedian or about your audience's sense of humor, play it straight—before you join the legions of unemployed comedians.

Spark fantasies

Frederick's of Hollywood, the internationally famous purveyor of lingerie, thrives on the principle that fantasies are more powerful than reality, that an intriguing promise is often more desirable than the naked truth. But how can technical documents offer an intriguing promise? The first step requires an appeal to the reader's imagination. We must make the reader imagine what it would be like to use the document and the product it describes.

Vicarious involvement

One way to involve the user is to present scenarios or case studies with which the reader can identify.

> The elation of her new promotion faded when Marian realized she had just three days to prepare an org chart, two financial analyses, a management presentation, and countless memos. She didn't feel any better when she learned her secretary was out with the flu.

The reader vicariously participates in the procedures and descriptions you present. Another technique is to use places and objects familiar to the reader.

For electronic tutorials and computer-based training put learners in a simulated environment where they can experience the same perils and triumphs as with the real product.

Spotlight the reader

Another way to draw the user into the document is simply to write the book about the user.

Make the reader the subject, the focus, the hero of the document. The secret is a simple, natural use of the pronoun *you*. Contrast the following two sentences:

✘ No	✔ Yes
The user removes the unit from the packing box and sets it on a desk, table, or work surface.	Remove your new monitor from its box and place it on your desk, table, or work surface.

Don't come on too strong

A heavy-handed or mechanical use of the second person is as convincing as a photocopied love letter. It lacks sincerity and sympathy. Such mechanical and formalistic use of *you* can be rude, fresh, and downright accusatory. For example:

> If *you* enter *your* number incorrectly the system beeps at *you* to alert *you* of *your* mistake. *You* must then re-enter *your* number.

Don't use *you* just to meet a Flesch reading-ease requirement or win a seal of approval from your style committee. Doing so will not win approval or acceptance from your readers.

Also avoid heavy-handed use of emotions, such as the generous doses of parental guilt often used in ads aimed at selling home computers to parents of school children.

8

PUBLISH SENSUAL PAGES

In an age of color TV and rock-music videos, pages in most technical documents seem like a session in a sensory-deprivation chamber. Stark lines of black ink on white pages carry monotonous paragraphs of dull prose. Not seductive. Seductions are sensual if they are anything. And pages in technical documents can be sensual, too.

A treat for the eyes

The reader can get the point of a picture immediately but may have to struggle for minutes to understand the same information embedded in text.

> A picture shows me at a glance what it takes dozens of pages of a book to expound. — Ivan Turgenev

And pictures break up ponderous columns of text, giving visual relief to the eyes and variety to the page. Graphics such as illustrations and tables are more interesting than bland blocks of text. Being two-dimensional,

they offer alternative paths of eye movement. Their main meaning can be realized at a glance and their details absorbed in a controlled, structured manner.

Display sequences in lists

Explicit lists make alternatives, steps, and separate items clear and distinct. We have several choices for how we present a series of items, depending on whether we are listing alternatives, instructions, or requirements:

Bullet	Numbered	Checklist
for choices or alternatives	for step-by-step procedures or rankings	for requirements
• Item one. • Item two. • Item three.	1. First step. 2. Second step. 3. Third step.	☐ Item one. ☐ Item two. ☐ Item three.

Figure 8: Typographic conventions

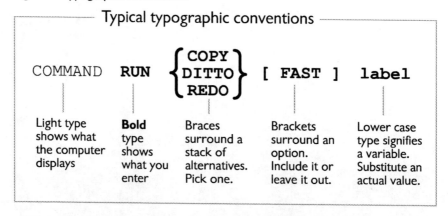

Typical typographic conventions

COMMAND **RUN** { COPY DITTO REDO } [FAST] `label`

Light type shows what the computer displays

Bold type shows what you enter

Braces surround a stack of alternatives. Pick one.

Brackets surround an option. Include it or leave it out.

Lower case type signifies a variable. Substitute an actual value.

Use typographic conventions to show rules

Consistent use of elements of typography provide a shorthand way of structuring information. Reference documents for computer software frequently use such conventions to show permitted variations of commands. See Figure 8.

Take care: the conventions familiar to you may not be familiar to your readers. Conventions familiar to computer programmers may baffle novice computer users. Even programmers have different conventions for different programming languages.

Muster complex information into tables

Tables can display difficult information in an orderly array of rank and files. As soon as readers understand how the table is organized and have read the headings and side labels, they can go right to the box that contains the information they need without having to read the rest of the information.

Head	Head	Head	Head	Head	Head	Head	Head
Stub	item	item	item	item	item	item	item
Stub	item	item	item	item	item	item	item
Stub	item	item	item	item	item	item	item
Stub	item	item	item	item	item	item	item
Stub	item	item	item	item	item	item	item
Stub	item	item	item	item	item	item	item
Stub	item	item	item	item	item	item	item

Whenever you find yourself writing a paragraph crammed full of *ifs*, *whens*, and *thens*, think about replacing the paragraph with a decision-table or selection table.

If the weather is ...		Then wear ...
warm	and dry	no coat
	and wet	raincoat
cool	and dry	overcoat
	and wet	lined raincoat

Use visual symbols as signs ... and hypertext links

Visual symbols are the ultimate in simplicity. Whenever you can create a simple and widely recognized visual image, use it to supplement words. Use symbols on tabs, in the table of contents, in illustrations, on maps, on covers and spines of documents, and in tables—anywhere words can go.

In electronic documents use such icons to jump to destinations and as emblems for confirming arrival. Here's a convention I have observed forming on the Web. Visual symbols for hypertext links are drawn as three dimensional buttons.

What courses do you teach?
Descriptions of ready-to-go courses that can be brought to your site.

Clicking on it takes the use to a destination where the same image appears flat this time.

Learn to draw

"But I can't draw a straight line," you say. Sure you can. Just get a ruler. And while you're at it, get a compass, a triangle, and some templates. You can even get software to let you draw on the screen of your computer. But there's something even more important than software and hardware: training. You've spent many years learning to write. Why not spend a few evenings learning to draw? Most community colleges have evening courses in basic drawing, technical illustration, and graphic design. Take advantage of them.

Don't worry if you can't manage complex, detailed illustrations. Often simple, hand-sketched line drawings are best. Even no-talent typewriter graphics are better than nothing.

Visual imagery

Even if you don't have access to an illustration, you can make your document visual. You can paint pictures in the minds of your readers. By using visual metaphors and images, you can make descriptions and procedures clearer and more memorable. Consider this description by a master technical writer:

> Some of the exposed snails were so masked with forests of algae and hydroids that they were invisible to us. We found a worm-like fixed gastropod, many bivalves, including the long peanut-shaped boring clam; little brilliant orange nudibranchs; hermit crabs; mantids; flatworms which seemed to flow over the rocks like living gelatin; sipunculids; and many limpets. - John Steinbeck, *The Log from the Sea of Cortez*. New York: Penguin Books, 1976, p. 60.

Remember, it is not the image on paper or screen that counts but the image created in the reader's mind.

Sweet sounds

Sensual pages do more than rustle as they turn in the reader's hands. They can convey the sounds of the subject. For example:

> When you insert the disk, it *snaps* into place. The drive *clicks* twice and then *whirs* as the information is read into memory. When all the information has been read, the *whirring* stops and the keyboard *beeps* once.

Imagine that you are writing for a blind person. Shut your eyes and try operating the product, using only sounds, vibrations, and physical switch settings as your guides as to what is happening and when to act.

Another way the sensual page uses sound is through language itself. Though readers seldom read documents aloud, most do subvocalize (read aloud in their minds). They are consciously aware of the sonorous flow and rhythm of syllables. I'm not suggesting that you write subliminal love poems to the reader. I am suggesting that you carefully read the manuscript aloud to avoid any harsh or awkward-sounding phrases and any erratic rhythms.

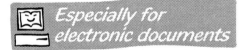

Of course multimedia documents can use sound directly. But you know that. And you also know that few multimedia documents use sound well. Too often it is used in an attempt to entertain or amuse. Users are annoyed or distracted.

In business and technical documents, sound works best when it is used to inform. Here are some examples of sound used to inform:

- Training physicians to recognize various heart arrhythmias

- Teaching auto mechanics to recognize problems with misfiring engines by the sound the engine makes

- Performing procedures that require looking away from the computer screen

Sounds that annoy or embarrass the user, fail. The user may turn off sound or reject the document altogether. To avoid such rejection:

- ☐ **Lower the volume**. Make the default sound level relatively low: slightly below the level of conversation in the user's work environment.

- ☐ **Let users adjust the volume**. If the sound is too loud users can turn down the volume. Often just knowing they have control is enough to satisfy many users.

- ☐ **Let users turn off the sounds**. Provide a preferences option where users can specify to omit non-critical sounds.

The intimacy of touching

In almost all cultures, touching is an expression of intimacy. The sensual page, through its texture and size, invites handling. It also invites the user to touch the product itself. It promotes hands-on learning.

Writing in the margins

One trick to promote involvement is to encourage or even force the reader to write in the document. Doing so involves the reader and personalizes the document. Some techniques for encouraging the reader include:

- Leave space for the user to write specific information such as serial numbers, account numbers, options, and switch settings.

- Label otherwise blank pages with the heading "Notes."

- On errata sheets ask readers to write corrections into the document.

- In tutorials instruct readers to write answers to questions and notes in the document.

Especially for electronic documents

Electronic documents provide more ways the uses can express their own ideas:

- Annotation facilities let users attach notes to topics.

- E-mail links encourage users to send messages to the producer of the document.

- Internet Relay Chat lets users hold discussions with the producer

Tactile involvement

More exotic techniques for using the sense of touch to involve the reader with the document and to communicate information include:

- Use textured paper for a luxurious feel.

- Use texture as the message. One ad for arthritis medicine used a sandpaper surface to suggest how an arthritis sufferer's joints feel.

- As a final exam in data communications I once used a jig-saw puzzle with one component of the system on each piece.

Active documents

Active documents are not so much read as operated. The reader manipulates their pages to extract information and in the process becomes involved with the document in a more active, personal way than with conventional documents. Examples of active documents include:

- Coloring books have been used in courses in anatomy, ornithology, and semiconductor layout. These high-tech coloring books combine visual and tactile experiences.

- Overlays on transparent or translucent paper can be peeled away to reveal various layers of detail.

- Scratch-and-sniff swatches are used to preview (presniff?) perfume and cologne. Natural gas companies have used them in pamphlets to acquaint homeowners with the smell of leaking natural gas. Such pages combine olfactory and visual information.

Multimedia allows even greater degrees of interactivity. Take care that the interactivity is purposeful. Let users interact with the document to navigate to specific information they need, to practice applying what they have learned, and to trigger optional displays.

BUILD A LASTING RELATIONSHIP

Seduction without honorable intention is vice. Seduction is not an end in itself. We don't want a one-night stand. We want the reader to do more than browse. Once is not enough. We want the reader to continually return to the document. We want a lasting relationship.

Lasting relationships are based on more than superficial affinities. Merely arousing interest is not enough. What is required is the depth to continually satisfy.

Honesty

No relationship lasts without honesty. In technical documents, honesty equals accuracy. If the reader can't trust the document, the love affair is over. One lie arouses suspicion; two, distrust; and three, abandonment. A document, like an unfaithful lover, has few chances to repair its tarnished reputation. Accuracy is a must. Don't take shortcuts with the truth.

The greatest danger is the inadvertent inaccuracy or the little white lie.

- Obviously posed photographs. No one's desk is that neat!

- Impossible scenes. In an early Apple Macintosh manual, a college student was shown mesmerized by something on the unseen screen. Macintosh owners were quick, however, to notice that the power switch on the back of the Macintosh was in the off position. The photo was not repeated in later editions of the manual.

- Omitted restrictions. Frequently brochures forget to mention that a software package requires unusual hardware options.

- Forgetting to tell how long a procedure takes or how much time must elapse between steps.

Openness

Openness means not hiding undesirable traits. Too often technical documents gloss over or fail to mention awkward features of a product. They pretend that the product has no flaws, that the software has no bugs. Tasks that the product performs poorly are often ignored totally as if the reader should never use the product to attempt these tasks. If flaws are mentioned, they are shrouded in legalistic gobbledygook. Many companies assume that confession is good for the soul but bad for business. Openness requires:

- Admitting limitations.

- Suggesting workarounds for problems.

- Showing how to recover from errors.

- Revealing shortcuts for tedious procedures.

- Documenting file formats and other technical details needed by advanced readers.

Growth

Without growth, human relationships stagnate and sometimes die. A document is a human relationship, subject to this same peril. How do we ensure that our relationship with the reader grows stronger and better? New content, that's how. We can publish revised editions of documents. We can continually add new material to our Web site. We can add deeper layers of material for those who have mastered the material in our early editions.

The secret is providing more content that the user really needs. Churning will not do. Merely rearranging existing content or making cosmetic changes satisfies few and confuses many. Keep asking yourself, "What else do they need to know?" And keep providing such information.

Commitment

The successful relationship results in commitments by the reader and by the document. The reader must commit to read and to trust what is read. The writer must pledge to guide and protect the reader. If these commitments are made and kept, the relationship can fulfill mutual expectations.

The secret of user-seductive documents is simply an attitude: you see your job not as putting words on paper or screen, not as putting ideas in minds, but as stimulating people to action. When what begins as flirtation flourishes as a productive relationship between the document and the reader, your documents will get the attention they deserve.

INDEX

CREDITS

Secrets of User-Seductive Documents was conceived and written by William Horton. The layout, design, and illustrations are by Katherine Horton using Microsoft® Word 97 and Macromedia Freehand™ 7.0. The text and headings are URW Galaxie and URW BlacklightD.

Deborah C. Andrews of the University of Delaware edited the manuscript and made valuable suggestions to the content.

Anita Dosik at the STC head office checked for dotted i's and crossed t's.